A Funny Thing Happened On The Way To My Stress Test

by Brian Gari

BearManor Media

Albany, Georgia

A Funny Thing Happened on the Way to my Stress Test
© 2012 Brian Gari. All rights reserved.

all inside photos: Jeanne Gari
back cover photo: Mackenzie Cathcart
design: Allan Duffin

for more info: BrianGari.com
email: garisongs@aol.com

audio version produced & engineered by Brian Gari
also available in eBook

No part of this book may be reproduced in any form or by any means, electronic, mechanical, digital, photocopying or recording, except for the inclusion in a review, without permission in writing from the publisher.

Published in the USA by:
BearManor Media
PO Box 1129
Duncan, OK 73534-1129
www.BearManorMedia.com

ISBN-10: 159393257X
ISBN-13: 9781593932572

Printed in the United States of America

Table of Contents

Acknowledgments	vii
History	1
The Clues Are Mounting	3
Angiogram	7
Here It Comes	11
The Deed	15
In the Interim (Jeanne's chapter)	21
Two Thumbs Up	25
Fall Risk In Springtime	31
Ding Dong Is Anyone Home?	37
The Last Day	43
Bye Bye So Long Farewell	47
Home Is Where Your New Heart Is	51

Acknowledgments

Dedicated to Jeanne…who probably saved my life.

Special thanks to my special editor…my mom

I would be remiss if I didn't thank the real life cardiologist (Olivier Frankenberger), surgeons (especially Daniel Swistel), doctors (especially Stewart Greisman) and nurses who got me through this ordeal…you are the real heroes.

To all my friends & Facebook followers who showed so much concern during this crazy time.

And to my publisher, Ben Ohmart, whose belief in my writing continues to warm my heart (even the 'fixed up' one.)

I
History

I turned 60 years old in February; I hardly expected any serious heart problems. I was about 167 pounds at a little over five foot 10. My diet wasn't bad (very little red meat). I did, however, get diagnosed as diabetic a little more than a year before (but on the low end, requiring two pills a day.) Yes, there was certainly heart disease in my family. Both my parents had bypass operations in their seventies. My mother had an actual heart attack and a triple bypass; on that day, I was called by the hospital and told to get right over. I will never forget my mother's words to me as she was wheeled to the operating room on a gurney. In true show biz lingo she said "If I don't make it through this, it's been nice being on the bill with you." How's that to bring tears to your eyes? She made it through. In the recovery room, she displayed strange symptoms. She swore I had flown people in from California to her New York City hospital and was keeping them in another room down the hall. (The drugs had made her hallucinate. She came out of it a short time later.) Her recuperation was fairly easy, given that she had had a mastectomy decades earlier that numbed her chest in the area of the open heart surgery.

My father, on the other hand, was a different story. He had had quadruple bypass and aorta valve replacement…one of the more complicated open heart surgeries. I can recall visiting him when he was right out of surgery and it was almost more frightening for me than for him. You see, when they bring you out of this operation, they have a tube shoved down your throat until they feel you can breathe successfully on your own. For him, it was a tube surrounded by cold air (oxygen?) and no way to communicate except with your eyes. I will never forget the absolute look of terror in his eyes wanting me or someone to remove this horrible thing in his throat that makes you feel as if you're going to choke every second that it's in. Eventually, it was removed. I knew it was horrible, but I hadn't a real clue how truly frightening it was at the time.

Both my grandfathers also had heart disease. My mother's father had two heart attacks and my father's father had had at least two. Medical advancements had not quite made the leap to help them in time.

So I was just sitting on a time bomb.

2
The Clues Are Mounting

For at least six months prior to my ordeal, I had had some pressure in the chest area, a little pain and a little bit of shortness of breath. It was all very minor and seemed as though it could be stress related. I was always having trouble with my cable company or landlord or both so I was walking around with a lot of anxiety and anger. Now don't get me wrong--I am not against those feelings. You would not be normal if you didn't have something that pissed you off in this life. So when I was walking somewhere, I felt this sort of anxious feeling in my chest...and it was happening more often than not. I am not one to dodge the doctor. I called for an appointment. I told him my symptoms and he did an EKG and listened to my heart. No problems. So I went about my life thinking what I thought before---stress.

My life was going in a more positive direction than it had in years. I got married again after being divorced for 24 years. I had met Jeanne quite by accident through our conversations on Facebook. It was October 15, 2010 that we finally got together. We hit it off right away; she was a nurse who was also hip to the music business having already been married to a musician. We really got along well and it was the first time in all those years that I felt comfortable enough again to ask someone to marry me. They say you just know and I think that's true. So we had a small wedding in our apartment and settled into married life with Jeanne working as a nurse and me continuing to write songs and all the other things I do in the business.

During this time I had gotten a call from a director in Maryland by the name of David Norman who wanted to revive my deceased Broadway musical "Late Nite Comic." I was shocked and thrilled. There had been no productions since it died on Broadway in 1987--the same year I got divorced! He said it would premiere on April 5, 2012 at Frederick Community College. Jeanne and I went there for the opening (and full run) and it took our breath away (perhaps a bad choice of words for me.) We had a great time at the show and in Frederick. It couldn't have been better…except for a little bit of those symptoms again. Why Maryland? Stress? Not really. We ate well and I even enjoyed utilizing the whirlpool in the hotel pool.

When we arrived back in Manhattan a few days later, I was dragging the suitcases up the subway steps (dragging is a good word) and was huffing and puffing. I had to stop. Seemed logical. Jeanne didn't think so. She thought I should call the doctor back the next day. So on Monday morning I did just that. My physician suggested that I call a cardiologist this time. I made the call right away and was set up for an appointment the following day. It was a simple interview but the cardiologist believed a stress test was in order. I booked it following my acupuncture appointment the next day. I had been going for acupuncture to try to get rid of the numbness in my foot caused by a recent bout of sciatica. The juxtaposition seemed ludicrous--a peaceful acupuncture and massage followed ten minutes later (I drove my motor scooter to make it on time) by a stress test. I arrived at the stress test smelling a little weird; my acupuncturist likes to use a eucalyptus massage oil that literally opens up your sinuses. The interns at the stress test said it got rid of the lunch room smell that had been permeating the office for an hour. They weren't quite sure which was worse. I got on the treadmill and began my stress test adventure. No big deal. I was told to tell the doctors when I felt those pressure feelings in my chest. At about five minutes in, I did feel a little of those feelings. They stopped the treadmill and used a sonogram (exactly like those that detect the sex of a baby for mothers.) The consensus was that I was to go to the hospital the next day for an angiogram. Meanwhile, I thought I could have gone further on that treadmill. Guess not. I asked what an angiogram involves. The cardiologist said they stick some dye through your groin up to your heart and if there's no blockage, you go home. If there is, they insert a stent and you stay overnight. I asked about how they go up through the groin and was told there would be some anesthesia and I wouldn't feel it. This was now getting a little scarier and more serious.

3
Angiogram

The angiogram was set for Thursday at 10AM in the hospital. Jeanne took off from work to support me even though I was insisting I could do it by myself. She wouldn't hear of it. I had some things I needed to send through the post office so we walked uptown and made that our first stop. Wouldn't you know I would be given a hard time on the way to this serious procedure? I had used staples to seal up one envelope and this bitch at the post office refused to mail it if I didn't buy postal tape and reseal the damn envelope. Fortunately, a supervisor witnessed the confrontation and scooted me over to a nice clerk who was happy to do business with me. (And the post office wonders why they are going bankrupt!)

We left there and continued our delightful walk up Amsterdam Avenue past the beautiful Cathedral of Saint John the Divine. Jeanne had to take some

photos, but I was growing more anxious and wanted to get to the hospital. She recalled that her ex-husband had some heart issues so she called him on her cell phone. He said he'd be glad to talk to me about the angiogram and stents. He told me it was no big deal. He had had several stents and was doing fine. "Don't worry…it's easy!" he reiterated.

ANGIOGRAM

We arrived exactly at 10AM and went to check in. We waited a bit and were ushered into an office where a nice, immaculately dressed gentleman welcomed us and went over a bit of paperwork. We were then directed to a room where my clothes would be put into a locker and I was to change into that famous hospital gown that never ties right. Already I was feeling like my life was being put into other people's hands. Keep in mind, it's not even noon and I'm getting very hungry since I was not allowed to eat anything since the night before.

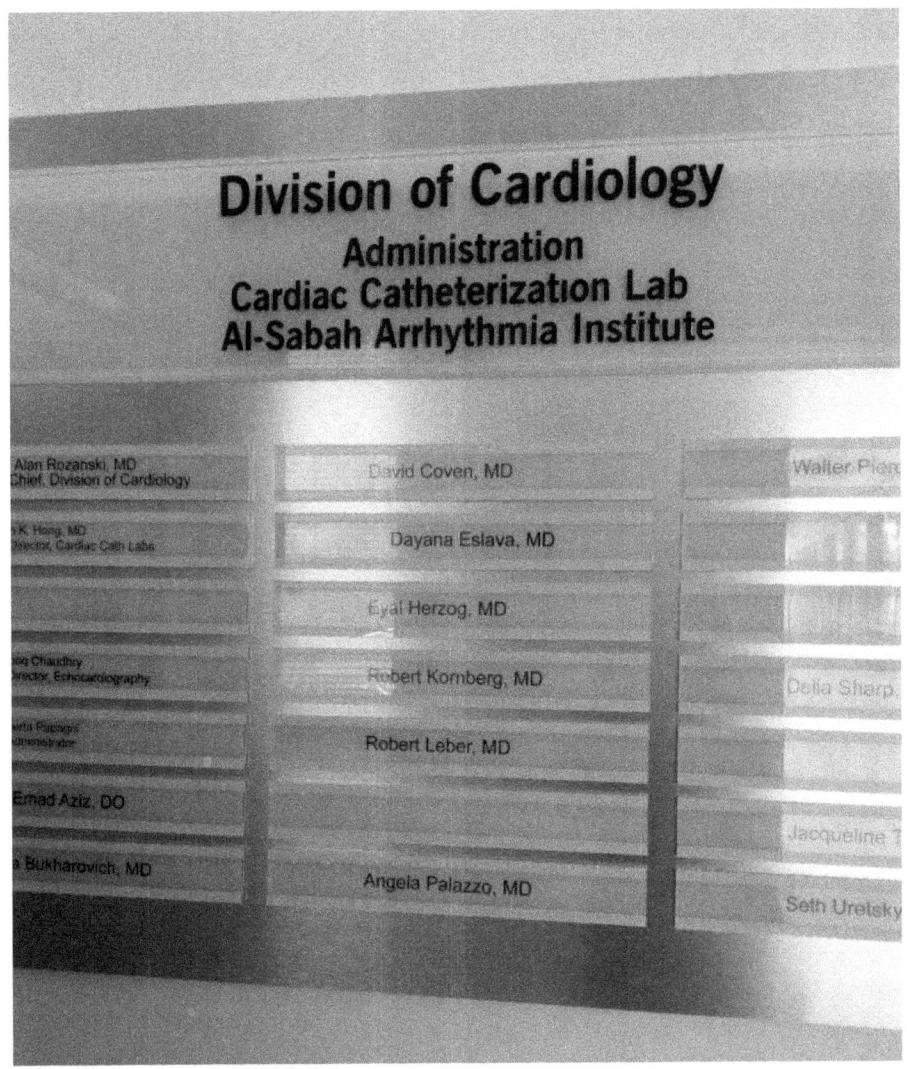

Finally, sometime in the early afternoon I was led to the prep area where they have to shave you slightly (no, not your face--I still had my beard) so they can get the area sterile for the insertion of the tube through your groin. They tried to put an IV in my arm, but they had trouble. The nurse blew the vein so she asked if she could try my hand. Fine with me. Just do it already. I am very squeamish when it comes to taking blood and inserting IVs. (Little did I know how many times this would happen during my lovely stay.) I recall being wheeled into the OR and it being very cold. They gave me more blankets (despite hearing that I would have to tolerate the cold germ free surroundings.) I looked up at the nurse and doctor and all the equipment and started to fade. My wife went downstairs for some tea, but something told her to go back up rather quickly. The procedure had been accomplished. She sneaked into the room where I was but was told by a nurse to stay out of there and wait for the doctors. The surgeon had to confer with my cardiologist. Everything was very suspicious. My wife was told the outcome and was crying. I came to and saw my cardiologist hanging over me and I asked him how it went. He said things are going to be a bit different from where we thought it was going. Oh? Yes…you will be having quadruple bypass open heart surgery in the morning. I was 95% blocked. I asked if I was going home that day. I didn't quite get it.

4
Here It Comes

I was taken upstairs to my beautiful room (I had no idea I was entitled to this, but I heard my doctors prescribed these accommodations.) It had a beautiful view of the upper west side of New York. I suppose if you're going through something like this, it helps the spirit to see beauty rather than pondering your fate. My main concern was food. Could I eat now? It still wasn't fully sinking in what was going to happen the next day. The staff was only too happy to bring me a couple of turkey sandwiches which I gobbled down very quickly. I squeezed out every drop of mayo & ketchup (and even mustard) from those stupid little silver packets they provide you with to make your sandwich a little less dry. I go along with the theory that it's a mayonnaise sandwich with turkey--not the other way around.

A FUNNY THING HAPPENED ON THE WAY TO MY STRESS TEST

HERE IT COMES

Little did I know, this was going to be my last solid meal for a while. There was nothing left on my tray by the time they came to remove it.

Jeanne and I were trying to come to grips with this news. I was going to have quadruple bypass open heart surgery the next day. Where was I on the schedule? Number two of two? Yikes. What do they do? Slice someone open, work for hours, seal them up and then grab me? I began to realize I was about to go through what David Letterman & Regis Philbin had done a few years earlier. I was younger than both of them (though not younger than Letterman when he actually had his surgery--he was only 52.)

Jeanne had called my mother and suddenly there she was in the chair by the window. No easy feat for her. She had been mugged five years earlier and has never fully recovered from being knocked to the ground and having her shoulder and leg broken. She has a hard time getting around and uses a walker or a wheelchair. But there she was supporting her first born in what was turning into a very major hospital visit. I bet she never thought this was in the cards. This was the first time the reality hit that I could die before she did.

It was evening by now and I begged Jeanne and my mother to go get something to eat themselves. They went across the street for a little while and brought me back another dessert. There was still this great Kozy Shack vanilla pudding waiting for me and now I had a rice pudding right next to it. I tasted a bit but couldn't eat anymore. I asked Jeanne to take them both home for me to finish up when (or if?) I returned.

I looked up at the TV and saw it had a message on it that you had to pay to use it so I skipped watching. It was the first of the bullshit in this hospital. I didn't find out until I came back to the room a few days later that the TV did indeed work and was complimentary---but no one told me that the first day. It didn't matter; I had my mother, Jeanne and a lot on my mind. I didn't want them to just sit around forever so I told them they could leave if they wanted to. I wanted Jeanne to catch a cab with my mom to make it easier on her. Jeanne was really in a panic despite putting on a brave front. I was simply stunned. I know they set this operation up fast so that the patient doesn't have a chance to realize what was going to happen. By the way, the next day happened to be Friday the 13th.

5
The Deed

I awoke very early to the numerous tests they insist upon doing constantly; blood pressure (the only test that doesn't hurt besides using a thermometer on your head), blood sugar and the inevitable IV. I was assigned a male nurse who couldn't have been more concerned; he was a very kind man who tried to calm me down with some very optimistic information as well as stories of his past. He really cared.

I decided I could get in one more shower. Why not? Be nice and clean for my operation. One thing missing. They don't supply shampoo. Jeanne called at 7:45 and I told her they were saying I would probably be taken sometime after 9 so she was rushing to get some coffee and race up to the hospital to be there when I was taken in. (All for nothing since they were way behind schedule but didn't let us know…I guess they couldn't leave the person before me 'half done.') I also informed her that I needed shampoo. She got there right away to make sure she wasn't out of the loop in any of the steps that were to follow. I thought my time was going to be at 10AM--guess again. It dragged on for hours. Do you have any idea what that wait is like? I am very glad I had Jeanne there, but what torture it is to know they are going to rip you wide open but keep postponing the deadline! It's kind of like awaiting an execution and getting pardoned every hour. And keep in mind, you are not allowed to eat or drink. I was glad I ate all those sandwiches the night before, but that can take you only so far.

I went into the shower but Jeanne forgot to put the shampoo in there, so I waited for what seemed like forever for her to return with her coffee. She had been on the phone with her mother and completely forgot about the shampoo. She handed it to me and I got back into the shower. First, I had a bitch of a time trying to get that damn bottle open. She had brought the bottle we took from our recent hotel stay in Maryland. She also didn't put her glasses on when she slipped it in her bag. When I finally got the bottle open and poured it on my head, it seemed awfully thin to be shampoo. That's because it wasn't! She had given me this blue bottle of mouthwash that was now in my hair. Nice way to start the day. Perhaps I should swallow some shampoo and comb my throat and have my hair kiss my wife. Don't want to waste the mouthwash.

One of the funniest things is when all the doctors on the case come in and line up like a photo shoot. They are there to prepare you for what is going to happen…sort of. They basically want to let you know you're going to be okay and will answer any of your questions. Most of them are not going to be directly involved in your operation, so it's kind of silly even to ask specific questions since they really don't know. One speaks on behalf of the staff and the rest stare at you like you have spots. And then they march right out.

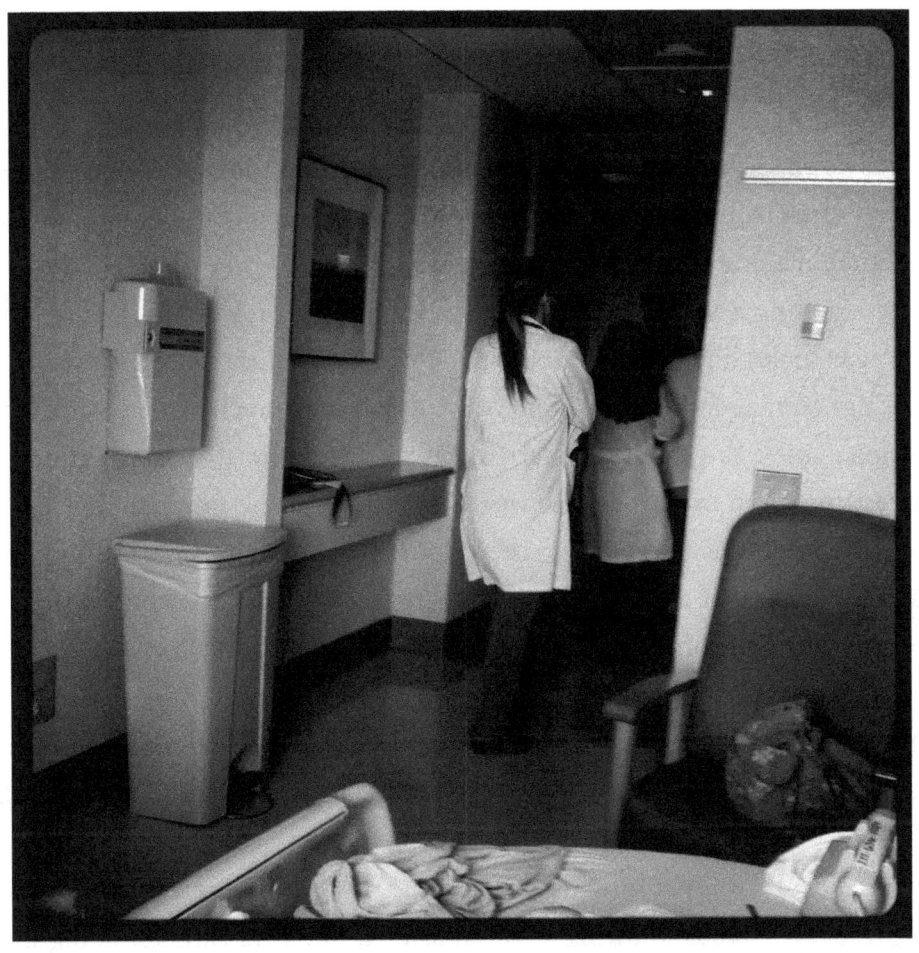

Jeanne took it upon herself to crawl into bed with me. Being as small as she is, it didn't take much effort or maneuvering. It was comforting and sad at the same time. We both knew how scary the next hours would be. It was 12:30PM and I still hadn't been taken to the OR. I was starving but was enjoying our last close moments together--in fact, Jeanne even suggested we go further but I told her she was crazy! She grinned and we kissed and awaited the executioners. They arrived at 2PM and said it was time. I moved from the bed onto a gurney and Jeanne followed. This was the start of my traveling by stretcher, and I must say it was the best part of this journey. I admit I'm a lazy ass who never exercises so to have people push me around on a bed felt great. I don't, however, recommend you get your body smashed to smithereens for a joyride through the hospital.

I was taken to the prep area, but this time it was for a more elaborate shave--all my chest hair. The guy doing it was very patient and considerate and took his time making sure it was quite smooth. I was a little nervous knowing it was getting a lot more serious now. Jeanne was very complimentary on my new look. She actually thought I looked good this way. This prep area was not even a room--it was kind of a tent within a much bigger room. The woman about to get my IV started was distracted by a woman screaming across the room from me. She was yelling that no one informed her loved ones that she was still waiting there to be operated on. She had a point. Most of us just sit around and wait and unless you have someone with you, no one gets the word if you're alive or dead. They finally calmed her down.

Now this is where it gets murky for me. I think I should defer to Jeanne as I have no real memory of what happened next--nor do I want to remember!!!

Jeanne: An IV was put into his vein to give him fluids. Next came the A line; I got really nervous knowing what an arterial line is (a catheter going into the artery.) It is very painful and I was wondering if they would let me stay with him while they did it; I was so scared for Brian. I begged the physician's assistant to let me stay. She did. Although she numbed him with lidocaine first, she couldn't get the A line in. An A line is deeper than just an IV in your vein. Although Brian was amazingly brave after much discomfort, they finally sent the anesthesiologist in, who told me, in no uncertain terms, to leave; I did. I was designated to the other side of the curtain. They gave him some anesthesia, which made him very woozy. I was so relieved as the anesthesiologist got the A line in. As they wheeled him back to the OR, I kissed him goodbye and stood and watched as I heard him say in this frightened innocent voice, "Are you going to break open my chest now?"

THE DEED

They looked at him with puzzled looks on their faces as he repeated …"is this when you're going to break open my chest"? At this point I lost it…I cried the entire way home. They said it would be over around 8 or 9PM; I looked at the clock--it was 3:30PM.

6
In the Interim
(Jeanne's Chapter)

I had to keep my mind off what was happening; I had my plan. I went out and bought two fashion magazines, went home and fed the kitties, put on my flip flops and actually sprang for a cab. (Sorry Brian, I know you'd hate that part, but you're sleeping.) I was just so anxious I had to get back to that hospital.

With a cup of tea, a bagel and my magazines, I was off to the 6th floor waiting area. It was a dismal room with a TV tuned to CNN that I hoped would keep my mind off Brian. What were they doing to him? I couldn't even look at those magazines. I paced the hallway trying to sneak a peek of something. Finally around 7PM my cell phone rang; it was our sweet friend Bronwyn wanting to know what was happening. She had gotten a phone call from someone who saw something on Facebook about Brian and open heart surgery! (Brian had kept up his Facebook posts through me and my iPhone--today's post was "Open Heart surgery today--film at 11:00")

"Are you up there all alone"? asked Bronwyn.

"Yeah, I'm okay," I replied.

"I'll be right there...I'm already in a cab," Bronwyn retorted.

Twenty minutes later in she strolled with her tinted glasses, a little box of pizza and two bottles of water. I was never so happy to see someone in my life. I didn't really realize what I was going through all alone and I'll always be grateful to her for doing this. She got my mind off things and we watched the clock together. I kept sneaking out into the hall to see if I could see anything. The CCU door kept swinging open and I would say, "How's my husband? Brian Gari?" They just looked at me. Finally, the nurse practitioner came out and told me I must wait in the designated waiting room. I kept peeking out the door.

After she left, I put a chair between the doors so I could see if any action was happening. I went out again and saw a sweet looking nurse who told me they were just closing Brian up. Oh my God, he was okay? It had gone well? He was okay.

Suddenly, the elevator door opened and I saw his face; they were bagging him (a hand-held device used extensively in the operating room to ventilate an anaesthetised patient who is not breathing on his own.) Bronwyn and I just stared at all the people surrounding his gurney as they maneuvered him to CCU. The table was surrounded by exhausted looking surgeons, nurses, physician's assistants and anesthesiologists. I said "Is that my husband?"

IN THE INTERIM

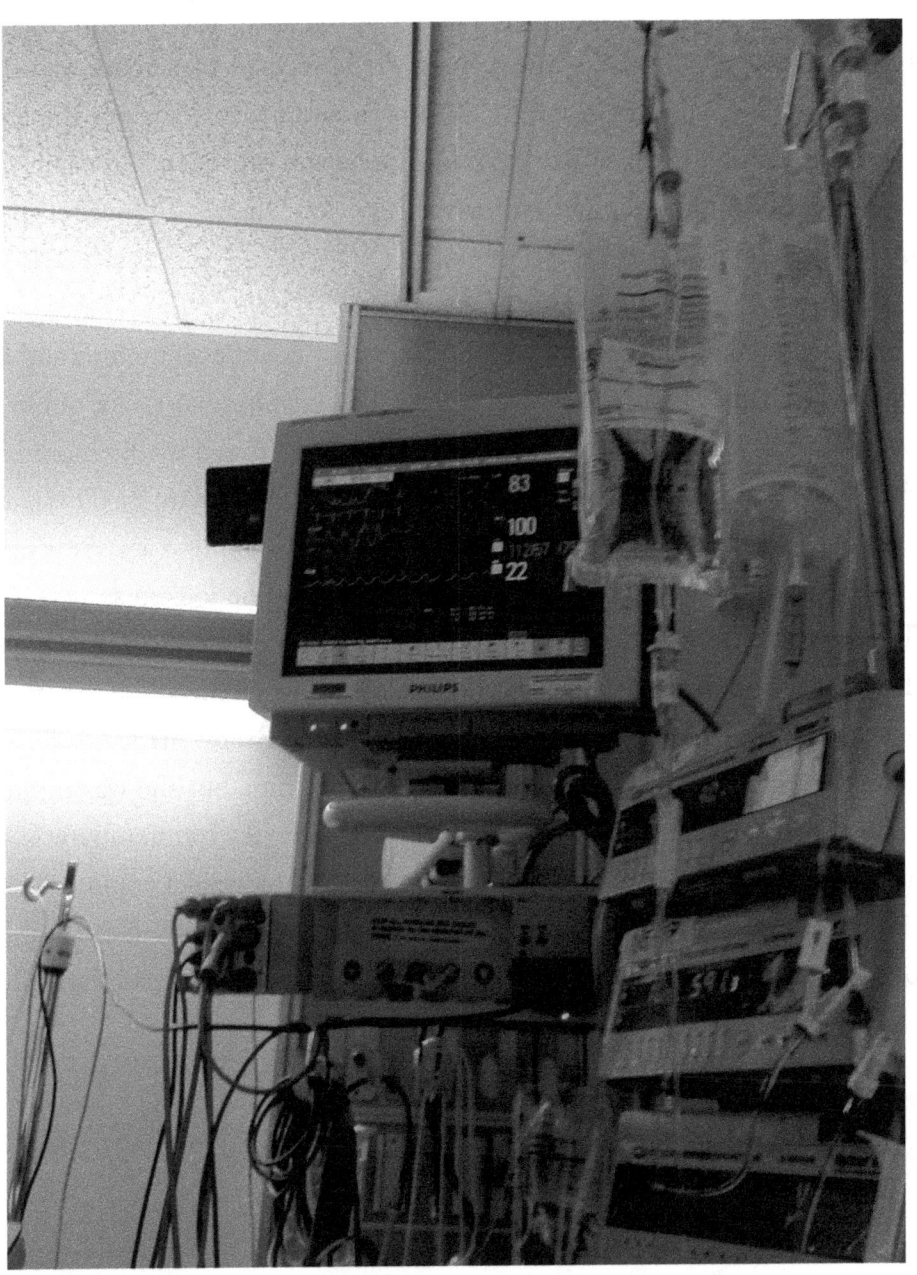

They said, nicely, "we'll let you inside in about 10 minutes…we just have to clean him up."

I was so relieved; Bronwyn and I hugged. It seemed like hours went by and no one was coming to get me. Bronwyn and I went out into the hall. I nervously stood there as Bronwyn hit the button on the wall causing the doors to CCU to open, and she pushed me in. Thanks Bronwyn…good move, because there was my Brian.

He was lying motionless in the bed surrounded by countless monitors and IV fluids with names I had never seen before. He must have lost a lot of blood because there was a full liter transfusing him. I was dazed by the monitors, the beeps and the ventilator. As a nurse, I tried to take it all in, tried to figure it all out. I have never ever seen anything like this in all my years of nursing. It was incredibly frightening. I looked at Brian and he looked so peaceful. They told me he would not be breathing on his own for the entire night. That thought frightened me even more. I kissed his forehead; he felt warm and didn't move. I just stared at everything as I felt Bronwyn's hands on my shoulders pulling me away. I didn't want to leave him, but she was right… it was time to let him sleep. It was so hard to leave. As I hesitantly walked away from him, a nice nurse gave me her number and said I could call any time of the night. I called when I got home, when I woke up in the middle of the night and when I awoke that morning. She was wonderful; each time she said he was sleeping. What a relief.

7
Two Thumbs Up?

I looked at the big clock on the wall and it said 8:20. I was completely aware that it was the morning, what I had been through, where I was and what exactly was stuffed down my throat. I tried not to panic. I must say the nurse (whoever she was) was right on the scene and knew what I needed. She told me she'd get the doctor and he'd be here within ten minutes. I knew I had to be patient and although ten minutes was seeming like hours, I also knew there would be relief very soon. I remember so little about this time, but I do know the doctor arrived right away and removed the tube from my throat.

I was assigned a nurse and I did not start off with a chip on my shoulder (actually that was about the only place there wasn't something uncomfortable attached.) I tried to begin with a good attitude toward my supposed caregivers. I was, however, in immediate agony in my back. What they don't tell you after surgery is that if you're flat on your back on a cold slab with your arms restrained for over four hours, you are going to have severe back pain. I was on morphine through an IV but it was not doing the trick. Some years earlier when I was hospitalized for herniated discs, they had me on morphine and it didn't do much good then either. This nurse had no concept of what I was feeling. The only words she had for me were "on a scale of 1 to 10, where is your pain?" I described to her that it was my back, and all she kept saying was "on a scale of 1 to 10…" Arrogant does not accurately describe this witch (a friend asked me not to use the b-word.) She also made it clear that I was going to go from the bed to a chair very shortly. I couldn't even conceive of this movement given the amount of pain I was in. She was very quickly becoming 'Nurse Ratched.' (If you don't know who I'm referring to, go rent "One Flew Over the Cuckoo's Nest.") She asked me to come to the side of the bed and pull myself up and stand. I could barely move. She wasn't about to hear that. She practically dragged me to my feet and I was in major pain. Forget the fact that my chest had been torn apart, my back was killing me. I got to my feet and almost collapsed into the chair where I stayed for the next seven hours. I couldn't conceive of reaching the bed again.

Jeanne arrived a short time later to see me sitting in a chair. She thought it must have been a miraculous bit of progress rather than a major car crash. Jeanne kept me up to date on all the wonderful Facebook get well wishes I was getting. It was so touching. I responded by saying "I'd send photos but I look like hell and I sound like Walter Brennan." I thanked everyone and also plugged my audiobook which I had just completed right before I landed in the hospital.

There was a TV in the room but no remote. Brilliant. What was I supposed to do? Jump up and change the channel while attached to an IV? They finally brought me a remote which didn't work correctly. It was a Zenith remote for a Panasonic TV. They said people steal the remotes so this is all they have--one that couldn't mute or change the channels. It did, however, turn it off, which is what I did with it most of the time. You can't believe how bad television is until you're stuck in the hospital. It's all Jerry Springer all the time.

I finally got back onto the bed at around 5PM. It was sheer torture and Nurse Ratched wasn't helping. She went into her "on a scale of" routine, and Jeanne witnessed it this time. She asked the doctor on duty if my pain medication could be switched to Dilaudid. Ratched changed it over at which time I got immediate relief…three hours worth! Jeanne knew from whence she spoke. I felt the medication drip into my IV and splash down the inside of my back in a beautiful calming cascade. I finally could cope with the aftermath of this operation…well, at least this part.

The bed was horrendous as well. I am fairly tall and these beds must have been designed by midgets. Not only did my feet go over the end of the bed, but they ended up resting on the steel end railing hurting my already sore bones. They also have buttons to raise it up and down but there is no way to reach the buttons from the angle one is placed in. To move one's arm to get at the inside buttons, you have to stretch your arm which is pulling on your painful chest. I couldn't do anything. AND to top it off, the button for the nurse was also dangling over the side so I could barely reach that as well!

Nurse Ratched went off duty (thank God) and was replaced by yet another nice male nurse. (Okay, would I like Heather Locklear as my nurse? Of course, but they don't exist so I'd rather a male nurse anyway if they end up being kinder than Ratched.) This guy was so understanding especially when he told me what I could expect for the next eight hours when I wanted more than anything to sleep. They were going to wake me almost every hour all night long. What is it about these hospitals and not allowing you to sleep? First of all, I was hooked up to a system where they can monitor you constantly but they still wanted to take your temperature, your blood pressure, your sugar, give you pills, feed you (and it was a boring liquid diet at this point anyway) AND even a sponge bath. I asked the nurse when they planned to do that. He said at around 4AM. Well I hated to disappoint him, but I explained I had taken a shower the day before and I would clean myself so there was no need for the wake up bath. He allowed me that pass and we worked out a little combination of some of the other interruptions. He was a gem.

As I tried to sleep, I was awakened every ten minutes by a loud crash. It seems that even though I had a plastic garbage can in my room, the room next door had a steel one creating a huge clang every time the nurses tossed out an empty can of soda. And if that wasn't enough, at about 8:30 one of the male nurses ran into some visitors he knew and decided to have a party--right outside my room. They were laughing and cajoling and wouldn't get the hell out of there. I finally called a nurse and said this noise is insane. I mean isn't this the time we're supposed to rest? It's bad enough that they will be waking you up every hour, but the few moments you can actually sleep are disturbed by a frat party.

My male nurse came back in to check my vitals and I impulsively asked a very strange question. I had been plagued by a vision in my mind of having a weird invasion of a very intimate part of my body during the operation. It's the only thing I remember from the operation. I blurted it out. "Is there any chance that some fingers might have been shoved up my…well you know… during the operation?" He very calmly replied, "you know I think that may have happened. I believe they insert two Tylenol up there to keep you from getting a fever or infection or something like that." Ah…so I wasn't crazy or having sexual fantasies. No one gets away with sticking fingers up my ass even if I am under major sedation!

8
Fall Risk In Springtime

I woke up (if you can call it that after being wakened constantly for either tests or just plain noise) to Nurse Ratched's return. She arrived with all my pills including laxatives, which are a staple (no pun intended) after an operation. Of course she wanted to know if they were working. I explained it will happen when it happens. Her response was "Oh no. I assure you you will poop before you leave here." I said "Oh no. I will go when I'm ready." She responded with some kind of threat that they will seek further methods if it doesn't happen. It kind of felt like Nazi Germany. It's a fact that pain killers like Percocet will really screw up your system so I tried to stay away from that drug. (By the way, I never did 'go' while in the hospital. I was on liquids most of the time.)

Speaking of liquids, there is another fun part of this operation. Somewhere during the prep (Thank God I don't remember), they shove a tube up your pee pee. Oh yes. They don't want you peeing during the operation so they insert a catheter to let you drain without using the bathroom. This is very convenient…for a while. When Jeanne arrived, she thought it might be nice for me to see her naked across the room out of eye's view of the staff. I yelled "Noooooooo!" My friend had told me a story about what happened to him when he had a catheter in him and suddenly got an erection. He was in total agony, so I convinced Jeanne that despite her good intentions, I was not in a good place for fun. Later on, I told Ratchet it felt a little like it was leaking so she felt she had to examine it. With my dignity out the window, she literally banged it around a little and then left the room. What she didn't tell me was she went to consult with the doctor, who said it was okay to remove it. She came back in, and without any anesthesia, she YANKED the unit right out of my unit! I can't begin to tell you (unless you've had this procedure) how painful this is. She gave me no clue that this was what was going to happen. Chalk up one more for the gentle bedside manner of Nurse Ratchet. I was still attached to an IV which continuously got tangled in the phone cord and nurse's buzzer. They gave me a bottle to pee in and told me of this toilet near the bed (which I could never lean over to even see.) Again, this bottle may seem like a convenience at the onset, but believe me, it is anything but convenient. It is so difficult to do something sideways that you are used to doing straight out (if you get my drift--again, no pun intended.) Eventually, I decided I would get up and use the bathroom dragging all these wires with me. They had put a wristband on me saying I was a "fall risk," but I laughed, believing that was like old people saying 'I've fallen & I can't get up!'

Because they knew I was a diabetic, they kept bringing me all those desserts (pudding, Jello) with fake sugar. I know I should not have sugar in great quantities (probably not at all), but let's be realistic--that fake stuff is crap— and I told them so. So what do they do the next time? Bring the same

FALL RISK IN SPRINGTIME

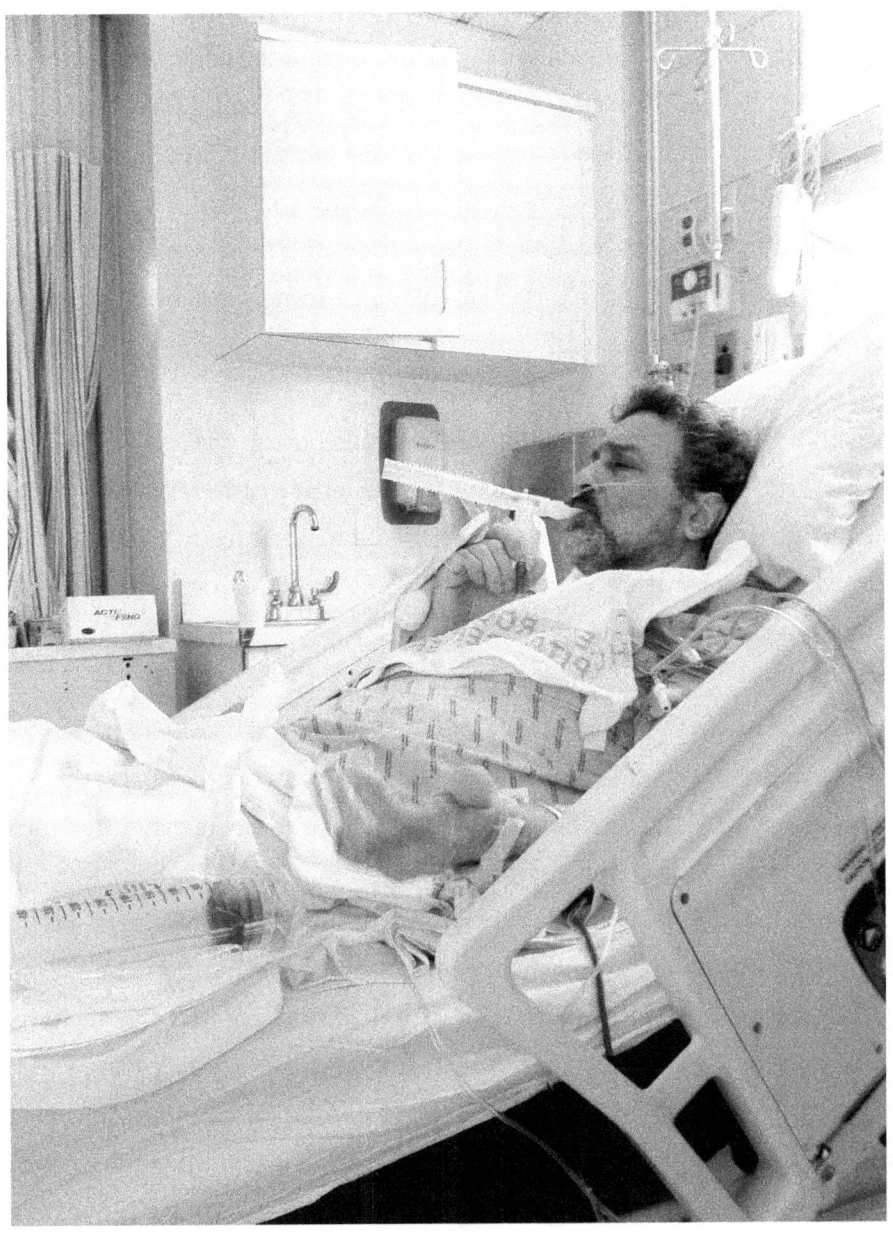

horrible stuff! I made it clear I wanted the real thing despite what my chart said. I was living on apple juice. They finally decided I could have real food again. And it wasn't that bad. Or maybe I was just desperate. I wasn't really hungry like I was before this ordeal. I could eat a lot back then. Not now. It was a challenge. I hated to leave anything. They had a jerk chicken dish with rice that I really thought I could finish. Not by a long shot. I would save these meals (more like hide them) because they had a habit of giving you a certain amount of time to consume them and then it was garbage time. I felt like a squirrel. I hadn't eaten cereal since I was a kid, but the Cheerios and Corn Flakes were actually enjoyable.

I was told I had to start using the incentive spirometer. That's a little gadget you blew into that is sort of like using the mallet at a carnival to see how high you can hit the ball. I didn't do very well with it. That really pissed off Nurse Ratchet who made it clear I wouldn't get out of there until I could reach a certain level. Yeah yeah.

Sometime later in the day, a nurse practitioner showed up. I had no idea why she was there. Little did I know what she was going to do. Again, they keep you guessing. First, she removed the bandages from my chest. I don't know what it is about these people with ripping off bandages, but they must have gone to sadism school. Now keep in mind, when I go swimming in a pool or the ocean, I like to work my way in gently--I don't just jump in. I have to get used to the water. Well, I guess these people don't have the time to wait for you to get used to anything so they just rip that damn bandage off. And that happened more than once because we get band-aids and bandages all the time in this place. Any body part with hair is fair game. Just grab a corner and tear. So after she was done doing that, it was now time for the meat and potatoes part of our meeting. She was going to remove the drainage tubes from under my chest. She was what???? Yes, they don't tell you about this little parting gift. It is necessary to remove these things and she was about to do it with, once again, no anesthesia. I panicked. My chest was incredibly tender; I had just been knifed and cracked and she was going to yank three tubes from out from under my chest. I didn't know what to do. I couldn't escape. She said "count to three and turn to me." "No, I can't," I said in a quivering voice. Well, she yanked them out and I saw stars. It felt as if she opened my chest again. Maybe she did. Because of this procedure, however, I had now earned my brownie points to leave the CCU and go back upstairs to my room with a view. That would happen the very next day.

In the meantime, I was stuck with Nurse Ratchet, the constant noise and the bed made for midgets. The second she left for the evening, I contacted the nurse on duty and asked if I could have a different nurse in the morning. She was surprised I had spoken up, but smiled as though she knew exactly what my reasons were. Nurse Ratchet was relieved of her duties with Brian Gari. I saw her pass by my room a few times and wondered if she really gave a rat's ass. I was proud I had the guts to ask for the change. It was worth it. Her replacement was very nice.

9
Ding Dong, Is Anyone Home?

Well, I got through the weekend despite the fact that sleeping doesn't seem to be allowed in this place. They continued to wake me up even though I begged them not to. I called in a doctor the night before and said this was ridiculous. I had no way of healing without sleep and the night nurses were so arrogant saying "they had their orders and no one told them different." The doctor said she would advise them otherwise. I thought it was all set. Nope. They completely ignored the orders and woke me about every hour. I was furious. I had to get my blood sugar checked (which was very high from the operation. I don't know what they expected considering I wasn't on my medication anymore.) They started giving me insulin shots and sometimes not in the arm. A new location seemed to be a priority--the stomach. Yep, a shot in the stomach. No, it didn't hurt that much, but when you see them coming with a needle toward your belly, you are in high fear alert! They also want to wake you up to give you pills, take your temperature again, do your blood pressure…totally exhausting. And keep in mind, they don't do this all at once---they come in probably every other hour so just when you fall asleep it's "knock knock…Mr. Gari?"

Now I contacted another doctor who guaranteed me I would not be wakened. I told her I'd believe it when I saw it. She couldn't believe the orders had been ignored. They actually weren't even written down. Whether or not that first doctor would be called on the carpet remained to be seen.

The replacement for Nurse Ratchet was lovely, considerate and helpful. Just goes to show what will happen if you buck the system a little. My surgeon came in with his crew, looking once again as if they were posing for the school yearbook or about to do a doo wop number. There he was out in front with his background singers to his right. He was great. He said I was coming along very well. He said I could actually do anything when I went home. Really? Yes. Just as he was leaving, I whispered to him "what about sex?" He said "you can have as much as you want." I thanked him for saving my life. He said, "Oh I was just the plumber." I was scheduled to do a benefit for the carriage horses of Central Park, and he encouraged me to do that and said he would have attended, but he truly had a prior commitment. (I actually did bow out myself because there were stairs involved and I wasn't quite ready…sex, on the other hand…)

I was told I was going to be shipped back upstairs to my private room with a view. I was back on the gurney for my ride to the 10th floor. When I arrived, my old friend, Michael the nurse, popped in to see how I was doing. He really cared. He also made sure my street clothes and belongings followed me because I had no idea where they went after I checked in that first innocent day.

When I went to use the bathroom, it looked suspiciously like it had never been cleaned. There were bandage wrappers in the sink and some piece of chipped plastic lying near the toilet. I mentioned it to the nurse, but nothing was done. It took several requests before anyone took a look; they apologized and went about cleaning it.

I finally lay down in yet another crappy bed made for midgets and tried to get comfortable when a strange lady appeared in my doorway. She was smiling like someone trying to convert you to a religion. She was, in fact, the religious lady! This is the person that makes it her business to visit everyone in the hospital who might need some prayers in their life. I made it clear (in a friendly way) that I was not religious and did not need any prayers. (Hey, if they want to help you out with a dose of religion, they shoulda been there when I was being shaved and prepped for the slaughterhouse!) Okay, she was very nice, but she saw she had no customer here, so she went on her merry way. She came back again two days later (that was her schedule) and Jeanne and I both thanked her for her concern.

Exhausted as I was, the parade of visitors did not stop with the religion lady. An old friend took it upon himself to pop by from two hours away in New Jersey. It was a real surprise since I did not encourage visitors. I looked like hell and needed to sleep so badly. We chatted (or he did) for a while, but I couldn't keep my eyes open. He offered to sit and watch me sleep. I offered him my leftover breakfast--a hardboiled egg and some tea. He took me up on it since he hadn't eaten a thing and I had had the cereal, which was enough for me. He was there for around an hour and a half, and I told him I really did need to sleep. He understood and bid me farewell. Just as I finally dozed off, the intercom system in the room blasted that they were looking for a certain nurse. This was the start of announcements all through the day and night. In this day and age, you would think the particular nurses they were looking for would have a beeper of some kind; not a chance. They found an annoying way of reaching them…using the intercom system in every room to locate them. I even got up to see if I could turn it off myself. No such luck so I called Michael, my friendly nurse. He and some others went about looking for a solution. It stopped for a while…but then returned with a vengeance. I asked a tech person who simply told me to call maintenance. He gave me the number, which I was suspicious would not work. I was right. There were more numbers to dial to reach maintenance. I got through---it was a phone machine. No one responded. One more piece of insanity this hospital had to offer.

I mentioned to Michael that it was too bad they charged for the TV. He looked at me very puzzled. "The TV is free," he replied. "You're kidding… they told me I had to pay last time I was on this floor." "Nope," he reiterated. "It's on the house." And with that, he clicked it on. Of course, I still didn't have a remote. That was like asking for the Queen to visit you, but Michael rounded up one that worked a little better than the last.

One thing that is a little disturbing is how closely you are monitored. They told me I was hooked up to a system that told them everything you were doing. Does that mean on video? audio? This made me wonder how much they knew about what you did in the privacy of your room. Do they know when you scratch? (or anything else for that matter!) They also pop in without any warning (oh yes, there's always that knock on the door--once they're in!)

There was a bureau with drawers right next to me and that's when I decided it was time to write down some of this lunacy. A friend of mine on Facebook dropped the hint that I would probably be writing a new song about my experiences. I knew a song wasn't in the cards, but a book might be another story (so to speak.) I searched the bureau. Not a pen or piece of paper. Maybe they knew. So I asked for the materials. What they came back with was a riot. One piece of hospital paper and a pencil so small, I thought they robbed a miniature golf store. I made do. I had no choice. The thoughts were coming so fast.

One thing you don't expect is the flood of emotions you feel. I started thinking about how my wife was almost a widow. What would have happened if I had dropped dead before the operation--or during? This poor girl had married only six months earlier and here was her husband hanging by a thread. And then there was my mother. What would she have done if I hadn't made it through? I was her first born and the only child still in New York. I don't think she could have coped. Tears started welling up in my eyes. Oh and my father. He went through this as well. I was wishing I could have talked to him about it. But he was gone. It made me sad again. I was grateful, yet depressed.

I realized it was past lunch and none had arrived. Yep, they forgot about me. I called the nurse and they said they would send something. It never came. I wasn't that hungry, and as I said before, I kept a little stash just in case. Nevertheless, it kind of sucked because at least the food would make my days a little more interesting. Oh, well. Perhaps I could count on dinner?

Jeanne was now back at work for the full day so I could only stare at the clock, hope for some sleep and count the hours until she arrived. I tried to use the incentive spirometer again, since they told me it was imperative that I make progress with it in order to be released, but I hated it and got bored with blowing into that thing. I would recover on my own time.

The doctors came by again and told me I would be released on Wednesday. They said I was doing very well and they didn't see any reason why I shouldn't make it home just fine. They believed I would recover much faster in my own environment and considering the lack of sleep I was getting there, I wholeheartedly (another pun?) agreed. I asked if there were any more "surprises" that might be disturbing (i.e. removals of anything), and I was so thrilled to know there would be one more--a wire attached to my heart. Oh, great. God knows what that would feel like. They swore it was nothing and certainly not as bad as the tubes. It put me into another panic. Just the thought of a wire being yanked out of that same area scared the crap out of me (well, not literally as I still wasn't "going." Too much information? sorry.)

Jeanne stayed for a few hours, but I was concerned about her getting home when it was dark. She had brought me all my newspapers, which I was determined to finish (including the entire Sunday New York Times.) I went through a ton of email and Facebook notifications. I answered a few but it was truly overwhelming. I kissed Jeanne goodbye and told her there would be just one more day there and after that it was home! She was pleased. I watched her depart as I was left to the hounds arriving with needles and whatever else they had in mind for my nocturnal interruptus.

10

The Last Day

Another night passed with very little sleep, but of course that went hand in hand with nurses being paged on the intercom system as well as checking blood sugar, injections and a bunch of pills. I was also informed that I would be having X-rays, but the time was a big secret. You can never get a definitive time out of anyone on anything. I was finishing up my newspapers when the parade of physicians arrived to let me know I would be leaving the next day. I innocently asked when that wire would be removed as well as some bandages. They said it would happen soon. As they all turned to leave, it was almost like a last minute thought when one doctor turned back, approached my chest and said he was going to take out the wire. Again, I went into panic. But he didn't wait for even a second; he simply pulled that sucker right out of my chest. It hurt, but not like the tubes. He said it was over. I began to think what other little gifts were hiding behind my chest wall. Maybe a hula hoop? an ice skate? No, it seemed they exhausted the grocery list and I was done. He walked away as if nothing happened. I asked a nurse if some bandages had to be removed if I was going to take a shower. They literally yanked a few off (which probably hurt more than the wire that had just been removed.)

I tried to get up the energy (and courage) to approach the shower. I thought it would be a really nice surprise for Jeanne if she saw me showered and dressed. What progress! I went into the bathroom and saw they had thoughtfully placed a chair in the stall. Nice move. I needed that. I looked at my body. Not a Frankenstein scar but not pretty either. There seemed to be holes in odd places (okay, keep your smart ass jokes to yourselves.) I felt like a victim of Bonnie & Clyde. I have no idea why some of them were there, but they were there all the same. They also have to take a vein from your leg and transfer it to your heart area for the operation. That in itself is not pleasant. It's gruesome to even think what they do and how they do it. All I know is you're left with a sore (and numb) leg which they say may or may not go away. I tried to wash off some of the orange dye that was somehow covering my leg, but to no avail--that stuff is permanent! With that accomplished, I waddled back to my midget bed and rested.

Lunch arrived, and there was still no time set for my X-ray. The X-rays were important to ensure my ticket out of there. I was afraid to doze off, because that would be the time I was to get on the gurney and travel to God knows where for the photo op. I got a call near 6PM; it was Jeanne, and she was telling me how she didn't feel well and asking if I would be upset if she didn't visit this one time. My disappointment was overwhelming; I was so proud of myself for getting all cleaned up for her visit, and now she was not showing up. I tried to tell her I had a surprise for her, but it didn't change the circumstances. She didn't feel as if she could make it. We would see each other tomorrow when she would come to pick me up.

THE LAST DAY

Jeanne's cancellation may have been a blessing in disguise. A gurney suddenly appeared in my room at 6:30PM. It was time for my X-rays. I was hoping I'd be returned in time for Jeopardy at 7. My hopes were quickly squashed. I got down there quickly enough. I had a nice little ride through the hallways and the overpass that connected the two buildings where I saw deflated Get Well balloons stuck between the windows.

I finally arrived at the "tombs," where the technicians were having a heated argument about some dumb thing. They looked at me and decided it was time for the X-rays. I said I could walk so I got off the gurney with my ass on display. I tried to hold that stupid dressing gown together, but it was a total loss…and what did I care if this guy saw my ass anyway. The first X-ray didn't come out. I was a little weak so I wasn't standing perfectly still--hence a blurred picture. The second time was a charm. I went right back to the gurney to await my chauffeur. The X-rays only took a matter of minutes so I thought there was a chance for Jeopardy. By 7:30 that chance had disappeared. So there I was…waiting and waiting while I lay there trying to pull at my gown so the passerbys wouldn't get a free show. It was now close to an hour since I left my room. I asked the technicians what happened to my "ride." They said there were only two people transporting at that hour and someone would show up eventually. After an hour and fifteen minutes, someone did arrive, and I went back to my room.

I was told if I waited until 10PM, they would consolidate my medications and I could sleep until 6 in the morning (where had I heard that before?) The hours dragged on and I tried not to fall asleep before 10. When it finally reached 10:00, I looked up--no one had come by. About twenty more minutes transpired and a nurse came in with all the pills and shots. I lay back and tried to fall asleep. Hour after hour went by and still nothing. For some reason, I started to recite Gerry Goffin's (Carole King's ex-husband & lyricist) lyrics. One song after another. I marveled at his rhyme of "trouble proof" and "up on the roof." This went on for hours. I just couldn't sleep. It's that old story…if I could just fall asleep now, I'll get six hours…five hours…three hours. Pretty soon you know you're screwed.

II
Bye Bye, So Long, Farewell

Of course, no one came in at six. Sometime around seven, they showed up with breakfast and pills. I asked them for more apple juice, and I hit the jackpot--they brought me half a bottle and said it was all mine! Jeanne called and said she would be over soon. I explained that my hour of departure was not carved in stone so she could take it easy. A male nurse came in and said he could remove all remaining attachments (mind you, the ones they put on me, although I wouldn't put that past them!) Of course, they yanked some hair off with it all. I got dressed in my own clothes and had to leave their gorgeous apparel behind (or is it my gorgeous behind that I left in their apparel?) I packed up everything including my secret notes for this book! I made absolutely sure I didn't forget those! I also took every toiletry that was lying around. Mouthwash, toothpaste, soap... you name it, I took it! Why not? They probably billed me 100 bucks for all that junk. They even gave me a teddy bear (which you're supposed to hug if you cough or sneeze.) Problem is when you have to cough or sneeze, you can't get the teddy bear fast enough--and believe me, you NEVER want to cough or sneeze when you're healing from this operation.

Jeanne arrived ready to take my hand and race to the exit. The nurses did not seem to want me to utilize the wheelchair for my departure. I made it clear that that is how I was going to make my exit. I was weak and this was going to be the last bit of pampering I was going to get from this place, so let's get the show on the road! A very nice nurse pushed me to the elevators and took me down to the lobby and outside. It was a very nice balmy day and all we needed now was a cab. Jeanne found one and I pulled myself up in the chair, thanked the nurse and got myself into the cab. I must admit I felt a little queasy, but it was a small price to pay for my freedom.

I hobbled into my lobby past my very concerned doorman and into the elevator where I propped myself up against the walls. I could barely stand. When we got into the apartment and into the bedroom, I immediately lay down on the bed. But much like my return after the herniated disc episode, I was more desperate to take a shower before lying all over my clean bed.

I had to use my old strategy for showering when weak. Gather up all the strength you have and make it quick but thorough. Have your shampoo plan in place and go for it. I did just that and landed mostly wet and naked back on the bed. I found some fresh clothes to don carefully. You can't be too quick when you have a very raw chest and a leg that is both sore and numb.

My mother came up, but I was not much use to anyone. I had so many things to catch up on. There were close to 200 emails (mostly from Facebook.) I felt a responsibility to answer most of them. They also sent us home with a million prescriptions. Jeanne had to get them filled. She called me from the pharmacy to let me know the cost of one of them--almost $200. I told her I'd rather die first. She was concerned and frightened. But I was outraged (of course not the best response for just getting home from open heart surgery.) But how can they do this to someone in my position? I could barely afford the insurance and now they want almost as much in medication? They had to be nuts. When she arrived back with the prescriptions, one of them was over $100. I told her right there she had to return it. I will not pay (nor can I afford to pay) that much for medication. I called my doctor and got an alternative for the time being. Jeanne also looked up on the internet how to approach the drug companies on drugs you need but can't afford. Letters and faxes went out right away…well, almost. My all-in-one printer/fax and scanner wouldn't work. Why not? Because this crappy company says if you run out of one color ink, it shuts down the entire machine from any other functions. Good idea? I think not. And just the aggravation I needed upon returning home.

My mother brought some food, but my appetite was not what it once was. I ate a little, but I was getting more and more exhausted as the night drew on. Finally, Jeanne helped my mother get a cab and the evening was over. I just had to sleep. I couldn't sleep on my stomach the way I had hoped and was used to--the pain in my chest was just too much. My only option was to sleep on my back and that I did….quite soundly for about eight hours..the most rest I'd had in a week.

12
Home Is Where Your New Heart Is

Waking up in your own bed is a blessing; waking up with a recently carved up chest and veinless leg is not. It all hurts like hell, but I was damned if I was going to take those constipating pain pills. Besides, I never ordered any. Jeanne stayed home from work for the first few days and deep down inside, I was kind of glad. I wasn't an invalid, but I wasn't in great shape. I would get tired at the drop of a hat (I hated when my hat kept dropping.) I did, however, make sure I showered every day. I wasn't about to become a disgusting recluse although I can see how you can very easily. We ordered out for dinner (usually Chinese.) It was sure nice to be home, but the healing process was going to be a trial.

A FUNNY THING HAPPENED ON THE WAY TO MY STRESS TEST

The most dreaded thing was about to happen. I had to sneeze. No time to grab a teddy bear. It just happened. OH, MY GOD! It feels just as if your chest has exploded. You have no idea how painful it is. I liken it to being operated on without the anesthesia. From that point on, I made it my business to NEVER allow a tickle to occur in my nostrils again. I would prefer a punch in the nose.

A friend gave us a beautiful present; she and her sister welcomed me home with a huge dinner that was delivered Sunday evening. It was an all Italian array of delicacies that was sure to please any of your taste buds. We were most grateful and had more than enough for several more meals. These people were among a handful that I could say truly cared. One thing you must be prepared for are the so called friends who may never be in touch after this major event. You can count your true friends on one hand. I have a friend who carried dozens of books up to my house just to make sure I wasn't out of the loop on the current literature. He called almost every day, as did a few others (maybe not every day.) Some emailed. But don't be surprised if some disappear…they do.

The following day I noticed we were out of milk. Jeanne wasn't around, and I believed it was now or never. I was going to make the pilgrimage to the local store myself. I showered and dressed and grabbed my keys for my first outing. (I even remembered to bring my dollar off coupon!) The doormen were shocked to see me as I slowly made my way out the front entrance of the building. I turned the corner and started up the hill to Broadway when this huge wave of gratitude overtook my whole being. I couldn't believe that a little more than a week earlier I was on the operating table being rewired in the most sacred of human body parts, and now I was actually walking by myself to the store for a container of milk. I had to stop for a moment to catch my breath, but I was determined to make it there and back.

HOME IS WHERE YOUR NEW HEART IS

I did exactly that. I was a little exhausted when I got home, but I was also incredibly proud of myself.

The next evening I pushed the envelope just a little bit more; I told Jeanne we should walk up about seven blocks to have some sushi. She asked if I really could make it and I replied in the affirmative. It was time for a dining out experience. I had thought the manager would appreciate our return. He couldn't have cared less. The place smelled of disinfectant, and I told them so. I guess that didn't endear them to me. The sushi was also extremely tiny, and they didn't take kindly to that either. Oh, well. It was still nice to be out. The walk back was a little tough for me. I had to stop a few times, but I made it.

I had a scheduled check up that Thursday, so my cardiologist said I should stop by there after the first appointment. I actually took the subway down (my motor scooter was out of the question, because if anything happened, my chest wouldn't survive.) The subway was okay, and I made it up the steps (and even stopped by the post office!) My doctor said I was doing fine (lost about ten pounds.) I was too early for the cardiologist, so I stopped by a Boston Market and had a children's menu of chicken, two sides and a drink. It was wonderful. I then headed over about another block to the cardiologist. I waited about a half hour and was finally ushered in. I told him of my aches and pains and numbness, and he said all of that was par for the course after this operation. He actually said I was looking great and ahead of schedule in my recovery. I walked over to the bus and headed home (damn--I missed the free return ride by only a few minutes!)

I wasn't home even a day when the bills started arriving. Yes, I had insurance, but surely you don't think that will be the end of it. Here you are trying to recover and the compassionless bill collectors are at your door before you even turn the key yourself! One doctor billed me hundreds of dollars for some visits to my room; Jeanne actually remembers her saying "Oh, I guess the other doctor got here before me," leaving immediately without doing a damn thing!

My major goal was to try to sleep on my stomach again. I wasn't getting the complete rest I wanted, so I made up my mind I had to turn over. Easier said than done. I cannot begin to tell you the agony of trying to do that. Even weeks later it didn't get any easier. Between the incision, the sore chest bones and the veinless numb leg, it felt as if no matter what I did, I was bucking the system. I forced myself to get used to it, because I knew that was the only position that would ensure some shut eye. It worked, but it wasn't always a guarantee.

I wasn't certain if the burning in my chest and swelling of my ankle was exactly normal, so I called my surgeon's office and the doctor who ripped out my tubes told me to stop by the hospital in twenty minutes. I hopped the subway, walked the extra blocks and made it there on time. I arrived on the floor she requested and thought it might be a place I had occupied before. When the doctor arrived, she had a big smile on her face. Keep in mind I hated this woman when she ripped out those tubes, but today was a different story. She was incredibly friendly and very proud of my status. I asked her right away if I had been on the floor before. She pointed to my room and said this was where I spent my recovery. All I remembered was ceilings because that was the position I was always in. What a strange feeling now to see other patients, knowing they would have to feel all the things I was feeling. She had me pull up my shirt and show her my wounds. She was thrilled with my progress. She went into great detail (at my request) as to what the marks were from. This was from this--this was from that. Some descriptions were a little bit repulsive even if it was my own body! She encouraged me to take more pain medication and sent me on my way. I couldn't believe I had survived all that. I also couldn't believe that was where

HOME IS WHERE YOUR NEW HEART IS

Jeanne kept coming every day and staring at me through the glass windows of my room wondering if I was making it. I asked the doctor one more question. "Was I really that close to death?" She replied, "You were in for a massive heart attack."

I walked out of the building in much better shape than I had that first day I was released. I walked down Broadway to the post office and then over to my optometrist. She was surprised to see me and being a religious person, made sure I was aware that God got me through it all. If she weren't an optometrist, I thought she could replace the religion lady at the hospital. I recalled I had a free bus transfer from the earlier subway ride, so as not to lose out on a freebie, I hopped the bus for about fifteen blocks to the supermarket where I did much too much shopping for this early in the game. Carrying the packages home was not as easy as I had thought it would be! However, it was still progress.

Clothing was also a concern. I realized very early on that certain shirts had to be eliminated. My chest could not tolerate buttons. If anything slightly touched the incision area, it was like a constant knifing. Hence, my eyeglasses on a chain had to be put in a pocket or thrown in a backwards position. I ended up wearing T-shirts or smooth soft cotton shirts. Jackets were not buttoned and could barely be zippered.

On another level, what seemed to be helpful was speaking to other "members of the club." I happened to get a message from one of my Facebook friends who had some giant hit records in the sixties. He was simply known as Keith, and he had hits like "98.6" and "Ain't Gonna Lie." I was completely taken by surprise when he mentioned he had had the same surgery eleven years ago! Inside of a few hours we were on the phone trading war stories. We had experienced many of the same moments that I have been writing about here. He said it wasn't long before he felt as if he had the heart of a

12-year old. It was that good. He joked that he recommends this surgery to everyone--even those who don't need it! Speaking with someone did help a lot. It wasn't that I felt I was the only who had experienced this mess, but I wanted to know what I was in for in the next few weeks (or months for that matter.) Keith's recovery had been quick, so it gave me some encouragement that this chest pain would eventually fade away.

I started to realize that the operation was actually quite commonplace today. I heard from friends and friends of friends who went through the exact same thing. They survived, and the doctors themselves felt that their work was more or less second nature to them. Although still a serious procedure, the operation was no longer considered a rarity--they are doing these every day.

One of my first evenings out was to see Neil Sedaka do a one on one interview at the Y. I had known Neil since I was a teenager and actually wrote the book for his box set of early recordings released in 2003. I also performed several salutes of his music where he dropped by and did a guest spot with me at the end of my performance. He saw me on line waiting to have him sign the book from the box set and kept staring at me. When I reached the front, he asked me how I was and I told him I was about a week out of the hospital having had open heart surgery. He and his wife showed great shock and concern. He wrote in my book "love you so." I saw him again later in the week and his concern never waned--and the energy from his music truly helped my recovery.

Little by little, I am seeing some progress. I can't say I'm ready to run a marathon, but walking up a hill doesn't seem to be a problem. Sometimes I tire easily and feel as if I need a nap, but I also don't sleep more than seven hours, so I feel I have a little leeway here. Oh, wait. I think I'm going to sneeze again. Oh, my God! Wait. Achoo!!! {pause} I did it. That wasn't so bad. I think I may be getting better.

www.ingramcontent.com/pod-product-compliance
Lightning Source LLC
Chambersburg PA
CBHW071501160426

43195CB00013B/2172